Naja
7/05

Everything
DOLPHIN

What Kids Really Want to Know About Dolphins

by
Marty Crisp

NorthWord press
Chanhassen, Minnesota

Edited by Ruth Strother
Designed by Michele Lanci-Altomare

Books for Young Readers
NorthWord Press
18705 Lake Drive East
Chanhassen, MN 55317
www.northwordpress.com

The dolphins in this book are referred to as *he* unless gender is known.

Photographs © 2004 provided by:
Corbis: p. 10; Corel/Fotosearch.com: pp. 9, 12, 20, 29, 38-39, 40, 51, 59,
60 all, 61 both top; Sue Dabritz-Yuen/Seapics.com: p. 55; Getty Images: p. 30;
Jeff Jaskolski/Seapics.com: p. 44; Frans Lanting/Minden Pictures: pp. 36-37;
Lori Mazzuca/Seapics.com: p. 48; Joachim Messerschmidt/Bruce Coleman, Inc.: p. 35;
Flip Nicklin/Minden Pictures: pp. 15, 25, 33; Michael S. Nolan/Seapics.com: pp. 50, 57;
Doug Perrine/Seapics.com: pp. 14 both, 47; Doug Pitman/Seapics.com: p. 13;
Xavier Safont/Seapics.com: p. 6 bottom; Sea World, Inc./Corbis: p. 52;
Roland Seitre/Seapics.com: p. 61 bottom; Shedd Aquarium/Liz Iammarino/Seapics.com:
p. 58 top left; James D. Watt/Seapics.com: p. 54. All other images from Punchstock.

Library of Congress Cataloging-in-Publication Data
Crisp, Marty.
  Everything dolphin : what kids really want to know about dolphins / by Marty
Crisp.
     p. cm. -- (Kids' faqs)
  ISBN 1-55971-049-7 (sc) -- ISBN 1-55971-042-X (hc)
  1. Dolphins--Juvenile literature. I. Title. II. Series.
  QL737.C432C68 2004
  599.53--dc22
                                                    2004002888

Printed in Singapore
10 9 8 7 6 5 4 3 2 1

Acknowledgments

SPECIAL THANKS TO DR. KATHLEEN DUDZINSKI, scientist-in-residence at Mystic Aquarium, Mystic, Connecticut, whose work is an inspiration and who looks amazing, even seven stories high on the IMAX screen in the 2000 documentary film, MacGillivray Freeman's *Dolphins*; to Stephanie Shipp, formerly of Dolphin Quest Hawaii at the Hilton Waikoloa Village on the Big Island of our 50th state, who took me "backstage" at a dolphin program and stood beside me in the water; and to Nina M. Young, Director of Marine Wildlife Conservation at The Ocean Conservancy, in Washington, D.C., whose comments and corrections helped make *Everything Dolphin* a better book.

Special thanks also to NorthWord's Aimee Jackson, an editor who sticks by you, and to Ruth Strother, who does her best (thankfully!) to make me get it right.

Dedication

To ROCHELLE "ROCKY" WELKOWITZ OF SOLUTIONS for Seniors in Lancaster County (Pennsylvania). In honor of your love of children and children's books and your work with people on the other end of life's cycle, who need somebody who understands and always finds time to listen. Thanks, Rocky!

—*M. C.*

contents

*We are drawn to dolphins
because of their playfulness,
intelligence, and sociability.*

introduction

DOLPHINS LIKE TO PLAY. THEY HAVE A reputation for helping other dolphins and even people who are in trouble in the water. And they always seem to be smiling. At dolphin shows, we laugh when they splash us and applaud when they leap into the air. If we're lucky, we might even get to look into their dark, expressive eyes.

Although these sleek creatures look like fish, they're not. They're air-breathing mammals, just like us. Scientists have studied dolphins for many years, but there's still a lot we don't know. As much as we love dolphins, we can't keep them as pets. But we can delight in sharing this world with such an amazing creature.

As part of my research for this book, I sat in on two assemblies given by Dr. Kathleen Dudzinski, a dolphin expert and founder of the Dolphin Communication Project. I listened to questions kids asked her about dolphins. I also talked to kids at various swim-with-the-dolphins programs. The answers to many of their questions are in this book.

If dolphins are mammals, why do they live in the water?

All life originally came from the sea. Some animals crawled out of the water and slowly adapted to life on land. Dinosaurs were the major life-form on earth for millions of years. When they began to die out, the plants and animals that made up the dinosaurs' food were available for other animals to eat. Mammals helped themselves. Some of these new foods were found both in marshy land areas and along the ocean's edge.

Gradually, some mammals, including dolphins' ancestors, began to explore farther out into the ocean. There they found a buffet of delicious fish. More and more, these mammals swam for their supper. After a long period of time, they adapted to full-time life in the water and became marine mammals. Around 66 million years ago, their populations started to grow. They eventually spread into oceans all over the world.

Dolphins, porpoises, and whales are all

Whales, such as this pilot whale (top), and dolphins, such as the bottlenose dolphin (bottom), are both cetaceans.

mammals called *cetaceans,* which comes from the Greek word meaning "sea monster." Dolphins are divided into two distinct family groups. The larger, more common group is the Delphinidae family, which are saltwater dolphins. The smaller Platanistidae family is made up of freshwater dolphins.

Although orcas are called whales, they actually belong to the family Delphinidae.

Dolphins are warm-blooded. How warm are they, and how do they stay warm?

All mammals are warm-blooded. They use part of their energy to maintain a stable body temperature. This gives mammals an advantage. They are able to move through areas that have vastly different temperatures. Cold-blooded reptiles, amphibians, and fish depend on the air or water around them to keep their body temperature stable. Normal body temperature for a dolphin ranges from 96 to 98 degrees Fahrenheit (35.6 to 36.7°C), which is close to the normal human body temperature of 98.6° (37°C). So how do dolphins stay warm in icy water?

Imagine that your winter coat is made of fat. Marine mammals do wear coats of blubber, also known as fat. The blubber insulates them from the cold water. Whales in arctic regions can have blubber that is 20 inches (50.8 cm) thick, whereas dolphins in tropical waters may have only one-quarter inch (6.4 mm) of blubbery insulation.

Porpoises and dolphins, such as these common short-snouted dolphins, are closely related.

How are dolphins different from porpoises?

Dolphins and porpoises are closely related. Porpoises have smaller heads and shorter snouts than dolphins have. They have spade-shaped teeth, while dolphins have cone-shaped teeth. But in modern language usage, some people use the words *dolphin* and *porpoise* as synonyms, both meaning the same thing.

How fast can dolphins swim, and how deep can they dive?

On average, a dolphin can "fly" through the water in bursts of speed reaching 30 miles (48.3 km) per hour. Dolphins can increase their speed even more by surfing a ship's wake, or path.

Human testing has shown that some dolphins can dive as deep as 1,500 feet (457.5 m). But dolphins usually stay within 200 to 250 feet (61 to 76.3 m) of the water's surface. This allows them to glide up for a breath when they need one. Dolphins are more like human skin divers, or free swimmers, than deep-sea scuba divers.

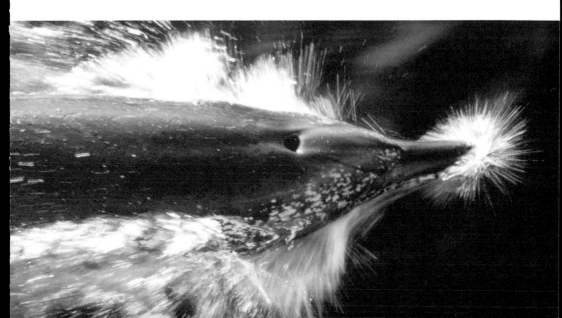

Do dolphins breathe the same way we do?

Dolphins have lungs, just like we do, and they fill them with air through their "nose," or blowhole. But that's where the similarities end.

It's funny to think of a nose moving around on your face, trying to find a better position. But that's what happened with dolphins. They started out long ago with their nose at the front of their face. To make breathing easier, the dolphin nose eventually developed into a crescent-shaped blowhole on the top of the head.

When dolphins leap through air and water, they are doing two things at once. They are breathing every time they're up in the air, and they are increasing their speed. Dolphins can move

Dolphins breathe through a blowhole on the top of their head.

faster through air than they can through water because air resistance is less than water resistance.

Like Olympic swimmers, dolphins exhale (blow out air) just as they break the water's surface. This is called spouting. Within seconds, they can fill their empty lungs with fresh air and dive again. But human swimmers are left panting after a deep dive. When we take a breath, we replace only 15 percent of the air in our lungs with fresh air. Dolphins are more efficient. They replace 90 percent of the air in their lungs with fresh air.

Humans don't have to think about breathing—it's automatic. We have to fight to hold our breath underwater. But dolphins have to think about breathing. They can stay underwater for 7 to 10 minutes. Then they have to remind themselves to swim to the surface for a breath.

Do dolphins have a sense of smell?

Not in the way we define smell. They don't use their blowhole (nose) for smelling. But they can taste certain chemicals in the water, which allows them to experience sensations similar to smell. Dolphins have no olfactory nerves, the organs humans and other mammals use to smell.

A dolphin's blowhole is not used for sensing odors.

How high can a dolphin jump?

Both dusky and spinner dolphins are especially acrobatic and can leap 20 feet (6.1 m) or higher into the air. In fact, spinner dolphins get their name from the spinning and somersaulting they do above the waves.

Who is the most famous dolphin?

There are two movie star dolphins: the characters Flipper and Willy. The movie *Flipper* was filmed in 1963 and starred an Atlantic bottlenose dolphin named Mitzi. It even led to a TV series. Flipper was played by five different dolphins in this series—Cathy, Suzy, Patty, Scottie, and Squirt. The movie and series were so popular that two movie sequels were filmed.

A remake of *Flipper* in 1996 stars Elijah Wood (also famous as Frodo in the *Lord of the Rings* movie trilogy) and a dolphin named Bebe playing Flipper.

The largest of all dolphins, the orca (also called the killer whale), is featured in the 1993 movie *Free Willy*. It was followed by two sequels (*Free Willy II: The Adventure Home,* 1995; and *Free Willy III: The Rescue,* 1997). These films star Keiko, a real-life performing orca. The films led to a successful Free Keiko campaign, and the captive orca was released back into his natural wild environment.

Sadly, Keiko, an orca like this one, died of pneumonia in December 2003.

Dolphins usually
rest near
the surface
of the water.

How do dolphins sleep?

We're pretty lucky. We can sleep without having to think about breathing. Our bodies take care of that for us. Dolphins usually rest near the water's surface because they have to keep coming up for air, even when they're sleeping.

Dolphins have two connected brain lobes, just like we do. Many scientists believe that half a dolphin's brain sleeps while the other half controls coming up for air. After a while, the working lobe gets its turn to relax, and the rested lobe takes over the breathing.

Dolphins have upper and lower eyelids and close their eyes when they're resting. Unlike us, they never fall into deep sleep, so they probably don't dream.

Can dolphins hear well?

Hearing is a dolphin's most important sense. Dolphins don't have outer ears, but they do have small ear openings behind their eyes. In addition to hearing, dolphins have a unique way of gathering information (bats use it, too) called echolocation. Echolocation uses sounds and echoes to pinpoint the exact location of an object. How does it work?

Dolphins make rapid clicking sounds—as many as 700 per second—called a click train. The clicks come from deep inside the dolphin's head, underneath the blowhole. Some scientists call this area (no kidding) the monkey lips.

You've probably noticed that the dolphin has a bulging forehead. It actually contains an organ called the melon. This organ is filled with a special liquid fat. It acts sort of as a lens, focusing the dolphin's click train into a narrow beam of sound. The dolphin's rounded, dish-shaped skull reflects those clicks forward into the melon. Dolphins are really broadcasting from the melon in their rounded forehead.

A dolphin's clicks instantly bounce off any-thing in front of it, sending back an echo. The echo

Hello Hello Hello Hello

Dolphins have excellent hearing.

is picked up by the thin bones in a dolphin's lower jaw. It is then passed up to a small pouch at the end of the famous dolphin smile. This pouch is also filled with a liquid fat and acts like a trumpet, magnifying sound. The echo then travels through the dolphin's middle and inner ears to the brain, where the dolphin processes the information.

What sounds
do dolphins make?

• • • • • • • • • •

Can we talk to dolphins?

Dolphins make many noises besides the clicks used in echolocation. They make creaky door sounds, high-pitched squeals, rat-a-tat clicks, chirps, whistles, whines, squeaks, groans, and claps. Some observers say that dolphin chatter sounds like laughter. Dolphins also make a lot of noises that are too high for the human ear to hear. So what's all the noise about?

Each individual dolphin has a unique whistle that can be recognized by other dolphins. Dolphins sometimes copy the whistles of other dolphins, as if calling a friend by name. And those dolphins who work with humans can learn to recognize both sound and hand signals, so we can communicate with them on a basic level. People, however, have yet to learn how to speak dolphin.

A scientist listens
to sounds made
by an orca.

What's a dolphin's favorite food?

• • • • • • • • •

What does a dolphin drink?

Dolphins are all carnivores, or meat eaters, and in the ocean, that means they eat fish. They like sardines, herring, salmon, codfish, shrimp, squid, grouper, and many other fish living in the underwater smorgasbord they call home. River dolphins, although also carnivores, have been observed eating fruit that had fallen into the water.

Dolphins get water from the foods they eat, so they don't drink. Dolphins have the same reaction to drinking salt water that we have. It would dry them out until they died of dehydration.

A grouper makes a tasty meal for a dolphin.

Are dolphins born underwater?

• • • • • • • • •

Do they have belly buttons?

Dolphins do everything underwater! About 12 months after mating, a dolphin mom gives birth to a calf who is about a third the size of Mom herself. A calf is born tail first. With no air in his lungs, a calf could begin to sink. But his mom and her helpers nudge him to the surface for his first breath. A dolphin baby sticks close to Mom, usually swimming right beside her to hide from predators.

Just like human babies, dolphin babies are connected to their mothers by an umbilical cord inside the womb. When the baby is born, the mother twists to snap the cord. A small part of it is still attached to the baby. Soon the cord falls off, leaving a belly button.

Do baby dolphins eat fish?

Baby dolphins nurse, just like other mammal babies do. They slide their tiny beak into one of two slits on Mom's underside. Then they curl their tongue, funneling every drop of rich dolphin milk into their mouth. In fact, Mom actually squirts the milk out so nursing can be finished quickly, in time for the next breath. In just one year, a dolphin calf becomes seven times heavier and twice the length he was at birth. A dolphin baby nurses for up to two years, gradually weaning himself onto a fish diet.

To hide from predators, this calf swims close to his mom.

Do dolphins have enemies?

Dolphins count some species of shark as enemies. Mostly, they try to avoid sharks. If necessary, a protective adult dolphin will ram a shark's soft underbelly with his hard rostrum, or beak, clobbering or even killing it.

And unfortunately, as much as most people love dolphins, we're their worst enemy. We pollute their homes, and people in some countries use dolphins as bait for catching fish. But the biggest danger from humans comes from factory fishing operations. They use nets that can snag every underwater creature that swims into them. These nets are intended for fish, but they catch dolphins, too. They trap dolphins underwater so they drown. The fishermen end up throwing the dolphins' dead bodies back into the ocean. They have no use for them. These lost dolphins are called by-catch.

The good news is that dolphin by-catch dropped from 100,000 dolphins in 1989 to 1,500 in 2002. Tuna fishermen now put scuba divers in the water around their nets specifically to free trapped dolphins.

How old can a dolphin live to be?

Among the many different species of dolphin, life spans range from about 12 to 80 years. Bottlenose dolphins live into their 50s and orcas into their 80s. In general, bigger dolphins have a longer life span than smaller dolphins have.

How small and how big can a dolphin be?

The smallest member of the Delphinidae family is the Hector's dolphin at less than 5 feet (1.5 m) and weighing around 100 pounds (45.4 kg). Hector's dolphins have distinctive rounded fins and are found only in the coastal waters around New Zealand. The largest is the orca, who measures up to 33 feet (10.1 m) in length and weighs from 3 to 9 tons (2.7 to 8.2 t), as much as a car or a big truck.

The orca is the largest dolphin. Some can get as big as a large truck.

Why do dolphins sometimes get stranded on land?

Dolphins lying helplessly on beaches are not trying to become land animals again. Mass strandings are still a mystery to scientists, but there are many theories. Dolphins are born with a kind of internal compass that gives them a reliable sense of direction. Instead of reading a map, dolphins "read" the earth's electromagnetic messages. If something happens with these signals, a dolphin's sense of direction can be affected. Other theories are that these dolphins may be affected by pollution or disease. Or maybe dolphins follow their leader in a fatal wrong turn. Whatever the case, groups of dolphins that get stranded can rarely be saved. But a single stranded dolphin can sometimes be helped.

Why do dolphin shows always use bottlenose dolphins?

Bottlenose dolphins are plentiful, adaptable, and agreeable. They're also a coastal species and easy to catch. Their natural curiosity, playful nature, and intelligence make them excellent ambassadors to the human world.

Do dolphins have necks?

Giraffes have seven vertebrae in their long, 7-foot (2.1-m) neck. Vertebrae are the bony segments of the spine. We have seven neck vertebrae, too, although they are smaller. And so do most other mammals, including dolphins. Saltwater dolphins have at least their first two neck vertebrae fused together, limiting head movement. But these short, stiff necks allow dolphins to torpedo through the water at high speeds. River dolphins live in more confined spaces and must be able to twist and turn easily. Their vertebrae are not fused.

Most mammals, from giraffes to dolphins, have the same number of vertebrae in their neck: seven.

What is a group of dolphins called?

Some dolphins stick together in small family units based on a mom and her calves. Some are solitary. There is no single correct scientific name for a group of dolphins. Names used to describe a group of dolphins include pod, school, and charm.

Several family groups joined together, as seen here with Fraser's dolphins, is called a herd.

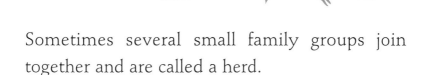

Sometimes several small family groups join together and are called a herd.

Lions gather in a pride, geese in a gaggle, and crows in a murder. It might be fun to call a group of these special marine mammals a smile of dolphins!

Can dolphins see well, and can they see in color?

Ocean-going dolphins have good eyesight both above and below the water. Each eye has a lens and cornea that help a dolphin make the change from water to air. Experts say that dolphins in air are a bit nearsighted.

When looking downward, dolphins have binocular vision. This means both eyes work together, giving an in-depth, three-dimensional picture. We have binocular vision all the time. Dolphins have it only when looking down.

Dolphins see well both in the air and in the water.

Dolphins also have an extraordinary visual ability to move each eye independently. They can move each eye up, down, forward, and backward, giving them nearly 360 degrees (a full circle) of vision.

Light penetrates only a few hundred feet underwater, so color isn't an important aspect of dolphin vision. Scientists believe dolphins cannot see color, although they seem to be more responsive to light at the blue end of the color spectrum.

Do dolphins cry?

Dolphins have no lachrymal, or tear, glands. But they have Harderian glands behind their eyes that secrete a jellylike fluid. This fluid helps saltwater dolphins see equally well in water and in air. A stranded dolphin is sometimes seen with thick mucus running over the edge of his eyelids. This looks like tears but is not an emotional response. It's a physical reaction to being stuck in air over a long period of time.

Why are dolphins always smiling?

Dolphins use body language, but it doesn't involve their faces. Because visibility underwater is often limited, dolphins don't depend on facial expressions the way we do. Over time, they've lost the ability to move facial muscles that would permit them to change their expressions. The shape of a dolphin's lower jaw looks like a smile, but is really an important part of echolocation. That's the real reason dolphins look like they're always smiling, no matter how they're feeling.

How many teeth do dolphins have?

The number of teeth varies by species—anywhere from 4 to 242. On average, dolphins have about 100 teeth. Dolphins get only one set of teeth—no baby teeth. The full set is present when they're born, erupting several weeks after birth. But they add layers to their teeth over the years, much as trees add rings as they grow.

Any animal with teeth can bite, including dolphins. But dolphins use their teeth mainly to capture and hold fish, which they swallow whole. Dolphins do not use their teeth for chewing.

Some dolphins
like people
a lot!

Do dolphins really like people?

Some do. Some don't. Some like a few people and not others. Wild dolphins have been known to swim up to people in shallow water to be petted and to get treats. Stories of dolphins coming to the aid of people in trouble in the water date back many centuries. But all of our information is based on such stories. They are not supported by scientific studies.

In the seventh century B.C., a Greek poet named Arion was robbed and thrown overboard by some thieving sailors he was traveling with. He insisted that dolphins rescued him. After that, it became accepted that dolphins bring travelers luck. The Greeks named the city of Delphi after these lucky charms. The word *delphi* literally means "dolphin town."

A more recent and well-documented example of dolphin helpfulness comes from New Zealand. Pelorus Jack, a Risso's dolphin, used to meet ships and lead them safely for about 6 miles (9.7 km) between treacherous rocks.

Jack continued his greetings for 24 years, until his death.

There is a lot more anecdotal evidence that dolphins help people. It ranges from dolphins towing lost rafters to guiding storm-tossed canoers. All of the stories suggest that at least some dolphins show compassion, not just by helping other dolphins but by helping people, too.

Why don't dolphins have hair like other mammals?

Actually, dolphins do have hair at one point. Dolphins in the womb have a line of tiny hairs around their upper and lower lips. These usually fall out before birth, leaving only the empty hair follicles. There are no reports of any researcher ever spotting a dolphin with a mustache.

What does dolphin skin feel like?

Dolphin skin is smooth and rubbery, much like an inflated inner tube. It usually feels cool and has a silky texture that is pleasant to touch.

Dolphins touch each other frequently in the wild. Their skin is particularly sensitive around their head, dorsal fin, flukes (tail), and flippers. They touch each other in the water with flippers and head rubs. In meet-the-dolphin programs, dolphins appear to enjoy having their bellies rubbed.

How smart are dolphins?

Being smart has something to do with the brain's size and its layers. Sharks are about the same size as dolphins, but they have brains the size of birds' brains. Sharks don't do a lot of thinking, unless it's about eating. The dolphin brain, on the other hand, is a lot like the human brain. It is large compared to body size, and it has many folds. Animals with brains that are big in relation to the size of their bodies are likely to be the "smart" animals. Primates (including humans) and cetaceans have the biggest brain-to-body ratios of all creatures living on earth.

Dolphins are smart animals and quick learners. Their brain is large compared to their body size.

Brains use a lot of energy. Animals who don't need a lot of brainpower don't have big brains. Even if humans haven't yet figured out how or why, dolphins must be using their big brains, or they wouldn't have them.

What are the rarest and the most common dolphins?

The rarest dolphin is the baiji of China's Yangtze River, which numbers fewer than 100. It is endangered because its habitats, or home areas, are being damaged by dams, pollution, and careless boaters. The susu dolphin lives in the Ganges River, in southern Asia. It is close behind the baiji with only about 500 surviving. Of the saltwater dolphins, the Hector's dolphin of New Zealand has only about 500 members left.

Bottlenose dolphins, the ones we most often see in aquariums and swim-with-the-dolphins programs, are the most common. They are found in every ocean around the world.

Dolphin sounds can be heard and felt underwater.

If you're underwater with a dolphin, can you hear him?

You can hear and *feel* his sounds. Some say that a dolphin's clicks feel like a shiver going through them. They say that the clicks fill their chest for a split second with an odd tickle. One researcher described the thrill by saying he felt like he was a drum being played. Another described the "touch" of dolphin echolocation as "a tingle on my skin."

How far can a dolphin travel?

Home ranges for dolphins vary. Dusky dolphins off the coast of South America have a territory, or range, of 580 square miles (933.2 sq km). But bottlenose dolphins off the coast of Florida have a territory of only 85 square miles (136.8 sq km).

Some stranded dolphins who have been rescued are radio-tagged and then released so they can be tracked by satellite. With satellite tracking, researchers have discovered that dolphins can travel enormous distances. One such survivor who was released in the Gulf of Mexico headed north to Cape Hatteras, North Carolina, covering 1,275 miles (2,052 km) in 43 days. Another traveled 2,610 miles (4,200 km) in 47 days.

Do dolphins fall in love?

Dolphins mate quickly, belly to belly. Both males and females often move on immediately to mate again. They don't show any feelings for one special dolphin of the opposite sex. Mama dolphins, however, experience an intense attachment to their youngsters and often travel with them throughout their lives. Male dolphins tend to find buddies and hang out together. Sometimes they join in a mating ritual with a pod of females, but they rarely stick around to help raise the kids.

Can people ride dolphins?

• • • • • • • • •

Is swimming with dolphins a good thing?

Although there are Greek legends about children riding dolphins, these marine mammals are not beasts of burden. A male dolphin in Brazil, long tormented by the local youth, is known to have killed one man and injured another when both men tried to ride him. A trained dolphin may give you a tow if you hold onto his dorsal fin, but this isn't the norm.

It's illegal to touch or feed a wild dolphin in U.S. waters. Observing dolphins in their natural habitat is a popular activity, though, along with whale watching. And recently, swim-with-the-dolphins programs have sprung up in the Caribbean, Hawaii, Mexico, Florida, and California. These highly structured and controlled programs use trained dolphins. Most of these dolphins were born in captivity. The dolphins

Education is the goal of swim-with-the-dolphins programs.

allow strangers to touch, pet, and even kiss them to please their trainers. In return, they earn rewards of choice fish.

Facilities that arrange meet-and-greets between humans and dolphins have one major goal in mind—education. They want to give people a chance to get up close and personal with the real thing. But the question remains: Should dolphins be kept for human pleasure?

Despite some opposition, dolphins have been used in amazing work with mentally and physically disabled people. Touching and interacting with dolphins seems to transmit a unique joy, the kind of medicine you can't get from a pill.

So are swim-with-the-dolphins programs good or bad? That's something each person must decide for him- or herself.

Many people benefit from interactions with dolphins.

What can I do to be around dolphins?

Jobs that involve marine mammals include researcher, field biologist, fishery vessel observer, laboratory technician, animal trainer, animal care specialist, veterinarian, whale-watching guide, naturalist, educator, conservation manager, and curator for a marine life specialty museum. Some artists, illustrators, photographers, filmmakers, and writers also work with dolphins. But none of these jobs include playing with dolphins all day.

You may spend long, soggy, sunburned days at sea as a field biologist or whale-watching guide. And sometimes you won't spot a thing. You may spend countless hours in a laboratory, operate on injured dolphins as a veterinarian, or haul buckets of smelly fish to feed your charges as a keeper. You may become an expert with a sponge and mop as you keep everything spotlessly clean in your dolphins' environment. In short, you won't be playing with dolphins. But you will have the rare opportunity to closely observe these special creatures in a way most human beings never do.

Dr. Dudzinski studies a dolphin in the wild.

Even with all that we know about dolphins, there is still much to learn about these delightful and captivating mammals.

meet the dolphins

Delphinidae is the largest and most diverse family in the cetacean group. Although experts disagree about the exact number of species in the Delphinidae family, all agree there are over 30. The following list of 33 true, or saltwater, dolphins comes from Dr. Kathleen Dudzinski. She is one of the foremost researchers of dolphins in the wild today.

Over years of contact with humans, dolphins, porpoises, and whales were given common names that are still in use today. As you will see, some dolphins are called whales. This is simply because that's what people called them in times past.

True Dolphins

Atlantic humpbacked dolphin
Atlantic spotted dolphin
Atlantic white-sided dolphin
bottlenose dolphin
Chilean black dolphin

Commerson's dolphin
common long-snouted dolphin
common short-snouted dolphin
dusky dolphin
false killer whale
Fraser's dolphin
Heaviside's dolphin
Hector's dolphin
hourglass dolphin
Indo-Pacific humpbacked dolphin
Irrawaddy dolphin
long-finned pilot whale
melon-headed whale
northern rightwhale dolphin
orca or killer whale
Pacific white-sided dolphin
pantropical spotted dolphin
Peale's dolphin
pygmy killer whale
Risso's dolphin
rough-toothed dolphin
short-finned pilot whale
short-snouted, or Clymene, dolphin
southern rightwhale dolphin
spinner dolphin
striped dolphin
tucuxi
white-beaked dolphin

There are also five river dolphins, all small (less than 8 feet [2.4 m]), almost blind, and rather slow compared to their ocean-going kin.

River Dolphins

baiji (beiji) or Chinese River dolphin
boto or Amazon River dolphin
buhlan or Indus River dolphin
Franciscana or La Plata River dolphin
susu or Ganges River dolphin

resources

BOOKS

BRIGHT, MICHAEL. *Discovery Channel's Dolphins.* New York: DK Publishing, Inc., 2001.

CAHILL, TIM. *Dolphins.* Washington, D.C.: National Geographic, 2000.

CARWARDINE, MARK. *Smithsonian Handbooks: Whales Dolphins and Porpoises.* New York: DK Publishing, Inc., 2002.

CLEAVE, ANDREW. *Whales & Dolphins: A Portrait of the Animal World.* New York: Todtri Productions Ltd., 1998.

DOBBS, HORACE. *The Magic of Dolphins.* Cambridge, England: Lutterworth Press, 1990.

DUDZINSKI, KATHLEEN. *Meeting Dolphins, My Adventures in the Sea.* Washington, D.C.: National Geographic, 2000.

FICHTER, GEORGE S. *Whales and Other Marine Mammals.* New York: Golden Books, 1990.

GUNZI, CHRISTIANE. *The Best Book of Whales and Dolphins.* New York: Larousse Kingfisher Chambers, Inc., 2001.

HALL, HOWARD. *A Charm of Dolphins.* San Luis Obispo, Calif.: Blake Publishing, Inc., 1993.

HEYNING, JOHN E. *Masters of the Ocean Realm: Whales, Dolphins and Porpoises.* Los Angeles: Natural History Museum of Los Angeles, 1995.

HOYT, ERICH. *Riding with the Dolphins: the Equinox Guide to Dolphins and Porpoises.* Ottawa, Canada: Camden House, 1992.

LEATHERWOOD, STEPHEN AND RANDALL R. REEVES. *The Sierra Club Handbook of Whales and Dolphins.* San Francisco: Sierra Club Books, 1983.

MEAD, JAMES G. AND JOY P. GOLD. *Whales and Dolphins in Question: the Smithsonian Answer Book.* Washington, D.C.: Smithsonian Institution Press, 2002.

NORRIS, KENNETH S. *Dolphin Days.* New York: W.W. Norton & Co., 1991.

O'BARRY, RICHARD WITH KEITH COULBOURN. *Behind the Dolphin Smile.* Los Angeles: Renaissance Books, 2000.

STOOPS, ERIK D., JEFFREY L. MARTIN, AND DEBBIE LYNNE STONE. *Dolphins.* New York: Sterling Publications, 1996.

WILSON, BEN. *Dolphins of the World.* Stillwater, Minn.: Voyageur Press, 1998.

WURTZ, MAURIZIO AND NADIA REPETTO. *Whales and Dolphins: A Guide to the Biology and Behavior of Cetaceans.* San Diego: Thunder Bay Press, 1999.

YODER, SUSAN E., AND MAJOR T. BENTON. *The Wisdom of Dolphins.* Naperville, Ill.: Sourcebooks, Inc., 2000.

WEB SITES

www.cetacea.org/
This Web site provides complete background information on every species of whale, dolphin, and porpoise known to humankind.

www.dolphincommunicationproject.org/index.asp
Log onto this Web site and learn more about how dolphins communicate.

www.dolphinlog.org
From the Cousteau Society, this Web site is chock full of facts, fun, and games. Click on Creature Feature to read about dolphins.

www.dolphins.org/
Learn all about dolphins at the Web site of the Dolphin Research Center. It even has a Kid's Page link.

www.nationalgeographic.com
Log onto National Geographic's Web site and click on Kids, then Creature Features. Have fun reading about a variety of animals, including bottlenose dolphins and orcas.

www.thedolphinplanet.org/index.html
This Web site is full of information and even has games and puzzles.

www.wilddolphinproject.com/index.cfm
Learn all about spotted dolphins on this Web site of the Wild Dolphin Project.

About the Author

AWARD-WINNING AUTHOR MARTY CRISP WRITES books for children and adults. She's also an animal lover and has worked for a veterinary clinic and an animal shelter. In addition to writing books, she is a journalist for the *Lancaster Sunday News* and has interviewed Newbery winner Phyllis Reynolds Naylor, literary legend John Updike, and has even covered concerts by performers such as Britney Spears and N'Sync. Ms. Crisp has four grown children and lives with her husband and their three dogs: Jessie, a Yorkshire terrier; Molly, a cairn terrier; and Sophie, a Cavalier King Charles spaniel. If you'd like to know more about Marty Crisp, visit her Web site at **www.martycrisp.com.**

Do you have questions about other animals? We want to hear from you! Email us at **kidsfaqs@creativepub.com.** For more details, log on to **www.northwordpress.com.**